THE AUSTRA
TERRACE
HOUSE

THE AUSTRALIAN

TERRACE HOUSE

BRIAN TURNER

Angus&Robertson
An imprint of HarperCollins*Publishers*

An Angus & Robertson Publication

Angus&Robertson, an imprint of
HarperCollins*Publishers*
25 Ryde Road, Pymble, Sydney NSW 2073, Australia
31 View Road, Glenfield, Auckland 10, New Zealand
77–85 Fulham Palace Road, London W6 8JB, United Kingdom
10 East 53rd Street, New York NY 10022, USA

First published in Australia in 1995

National Library of Australia
Cataloguing-in-Publication data:

Turner, Brian (Brian Ernest), 1940– .
    The Australian terrace house.

    ISBN 0 207 18663 4

    1. Terrace houses — Australia. 2 Architecture, Domestic —
    Australia. 3. Dwellings — Australia. I. Title.
728.3120994

Cover photograph by Brian Turner
Designed by Kerry Klinner
Printed in Hong Kong

9 8 7 6 5 4 3 2 1
98 97 96 95

Dedicated to the late Sali Herman

✦✦✦

*I painted houses because houses are parts of people
and people are parts of houses.*

SALI HERMAN, 1958

CONTENTS

INTRODUCTION

Whole blocks from street to street were covered with these vertebrated buildings.
The street front had a two-storey cast-iron dipped verandah, capped by an ornamental parapet
with an urn sitting atop each party wall.

ROBIN BOYD, 'THE BOOM STYLE', *AUSTRALIA'S HOME*, 1952

PREVIOUS PAGE ◆ *Louisa Terrace, at 71 Drummond Street, Carlton, in Melbourne, was originally a pair of joined houses. The house on the right had its entrance around the corner. It is an example of what was considered the minimum number of houses to which the word 'terrace' could be applied. Today, definitions and uses are a little more relaxed. It has been successfully converted into a restaurant without its dainty 1873 exterior being harmed.*

Most Australian terrace houses have passed their one hundredth birthday. During those one hundred years, they have undergone a cycle of fashion, decline and renewal, and their status and value have fluctuated wildly. They were highly fashionable during the late nineteenth century, their 'boom' period, when most of the terraces we see today were first built, but they were quickly abandoned when architectural fashions changed. For the first half of the twentieth century most terrace house areas were decrepit and the word 'terrace' carried a slum stigma. Now, in the latter part of this century, they are much sought after once again and have been subject to some of the most extra-ordinary increases in real estate values this country has seen. These days, tourist buses cruise the streets of Sydney's Paddington and Melbourne's Albert Park to view Victorian-era streetscapes that are amongst the most intact in the world.

Terrace houses are more loved now than when they were first built; the retrospect of one hundred years has cast a forgiving glow over some of the shortcomings of these splendidly symmetrical rows of houses. Of course, indifference to and the underrating of the recent past is not an attitude unique to Australians. For example, in England some brutal demolitions of ter-races during the 1930s were followed by the even more savage 'blitzing' of the 1940s during the

LEFT ◆ *This picture, taken in Ballarat in 1875, conveys a sense of prosperity, confidence and pride of ownership. A terrace house was a measure of its owners' social status. The overly effusive use of ornament contributed to the terrace's downfall at the end of the nineteenth century, but that same quality has also been one of the reasons for its redemption in the latter decades of this century. Today, the ever-increasing value of a beautifully restored terrace house is again a measure of prosperity and prestige. The cycle of fashion has turned a full circle. And a terrace house, painstakingly restored, is also a clear indication of its owner's respect for Australia's architectural heritage.*

Second World War. John Summerson, in his 1947 classic, *Georgian London*, was indifferent to the Regency terraces of John Nash, describing them as 'sham ... flagrant and absurd', but mellowed to say:

> The truth is that these buildings, careless and clumsy though they are in many ways, have an extravagant scenic character which, perceived through the nostalgic mists of time, makes them irresistible.

This book is meant as a portrait of the faces that Australian terrace houses present to the street. It seeks to portray the stylistic variety of terrace house facades. In doing this, I focus on their detailing, ornament and motifs, on the materials used, and on regional differences. I have not described what lies behind those

ABOVE ◆ *Palmette pattern on the balusters of the Marine Residences in Adelaide. These imported panels bear the mark of a Glasgow foundry, but are also listed in the catalogues that were published by the Adelaide foundries G. Fulton and Co. and Stewart and Harley 'Sun' Foundry.*

facades, and so the book does not cover terrace layout, plans, restoration or interior decoration. These subjects are worthy of separate books in themselves.

The terrace is the most enduring of Australia's architectural styles. 'Born-again' terrace houses that have been restored to their original state have become a distinctive feature, in the late twentieth century, of Australian cities and older towns. They are illustrated throughout this book. I have selected examples of both the grandiose and the minuscule, the unique and the commonplace, the inner city and the provincial, to convey an overall picture of their variety of detail and stylistic exuberance.

The term 'terrace house' is an overworked one, and used capriciously in Australia. It is used to describe all old, joined houses that have either separate or shared walls. It is also used to describe a pair of 'semi-detached' houses. And the contradictions implied in the expression 'free-standing terrace' are simply overlooked as this term also gains currency. Theoretically, the minimum number of joined houses needed to form a terrace is three. But nineteenth-century builders saw fit to add the appellation 'terrace' to some pairs of semi-detached houses, such as Ellen's Terrace (see page 2) or Louisa Terrace (see page 8), so I feel that no further justification is required for the inclusion of such houses in this book.

LEFT ◆ *'The galvanised-iron roofs on their front verandahs dipped in a sudden curve like the brim of a sundowner's hat and were draped at the edges with cast iron, like corks on the brim to frighten away flies.'*
Robin Boyd
Australia's Home, 1952.
Robin Boyd's whimsical description of late nineteenth-century balconies is particularly apt for the striped balcony canopy and fringe of cast iron of this restored terrace house at 50 Gipps Street, Paddington. It has been painted in traditional Victorian colours.

BELOW ◆ *Elegant polychrome brickwork adds interest to the chimney of a Melbourne terrace.*

Pedants may argue for 'terraced house' instead of 'terrace house', but Australians find that term portentous. Turning to the *Macquarie Dictionary* as arbiter, where a terrace is defined as 'a row of identical houses, or a house in such a row', I have used 'terrace' in this book to describe a row of houses as a cohesive whole and 'terrace house' as a house in such a row. I have also taken the liberty of sometimes using 'terrace' to describe either a row or an individual house when the meaning is abundantly clear from the context or the picture. Free-standing houses that have the character of terrace houses have also been included in the scope of this book.

Finally, I must thank those who have ultimately made this book possible — the owners of Australia's terrace houses. Many have lavished much time, love, attention and enormous amounts of money to restore their homes to their original state. These houses now enrich our inner-city streetscapes, reminders of the freshness, confidence, the excess of ornamentation and display, and the sheer exuberance, that was the Victorian era — an era that bequeathed to Australia this distinctive and enduring architectural style.

RIGHT ✦ *Terrace-style houses had wide appeal during the late nineteenth century and were also built on large blocks of land as free-standing houses, with windows along their side walls. They were especially popular in country centres such as Ballarat and Bathurst. This double-storey house, Afton, in Mudgee, New South Wales, has all the characteristics of a terrace. The iron-lace pattern on its balcony is not seen elsewhere. And despite the inherent contradictions, the term 'free-standing terrace' seems to be entering the vocabulary.*

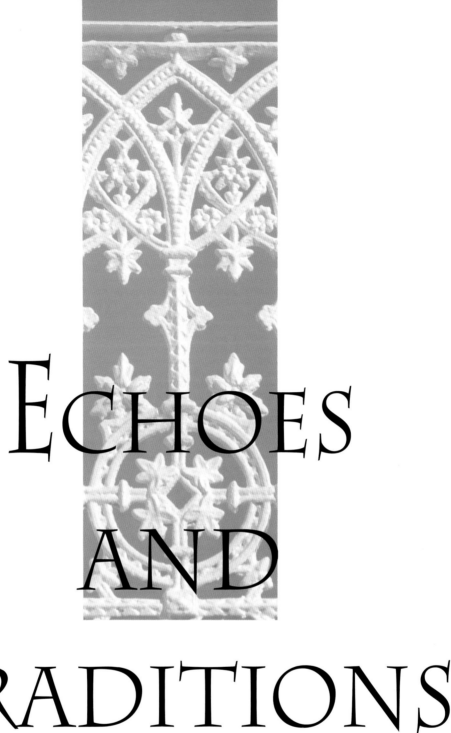

ECHOES AND TRADITIONS

'A pity that you huddle', said the German. 'Your country is of great subtlety.'

PATRICK WHITE, *VOSS*, 1957

A New Landscape,
an Old Architecture

✦ ✦ ✦

PREVIOUS PAGE ✦ *Clarendon Terrace, East Melbourne, was built in 1857 for wine merchant, Charles Lester. The three houses were designed to resemble a single Classical mansion, the central house having a splendid portico of Corinthian columns.*

When the First Fleet dropped anchor at the edge of this vast and expansive continent in 1788, the notions that Captain Phillip, the Governor of the new colony, had about living space and area were still very much within the cramped terms of Georgian-era London and Bath. By 1789 the 1000 inhabitants of the settlement at Sydney Cove had huddled together in an area no bigger than 1 square kilometre.

ABOVE ✦ *Cavendish Crescent (1817–23), in Bath, England, with Lansdown Crescent (1789–93) to the right.*

The English cities that existed in the memories of the First Fleeters — Hogarthian London street scenes in the case of many of the convicts, and elegant Bath terraces for Phillip, who had visited his aunts there to farewell them before sailing for Australia — were cities of terraces.

The concept of joined houses sharing a common wall is an old one and can be seen in Pompeii and in walled medieval cities in Europe. The device of combining these separate houses into a single handsome terrace building was refined in England during the Georgian era.

From the 1760s to 1830 English architects such as the Adam brothers and John Nash were responsible for creating the splendid London vistas of sweeps of tall, narrow-fronted houses, designed to resemble one wide and stately mansion. The Adam's Adelphi was the first to have the term 'terras' applied to it to describe its unified row of houses, sharing common walls and a cohesive frontage.[1] The remarkable John Nash was in his seventies when he designed most of

ABOVE ◆ *A row of Regency terraces in Millbank, London. Features such as iron palisade fences and cast-iron balconies as seen here were later repeated and then enlarged upon in Sydney. The colonial architect John Verge perhaps had buildings such as these in mind when he designed terraces as townhouses for his clients in Sydney (see pages 24–25).*

his terraces. His magnificent Carlton House Terrace, begun in 1827, was criticised by architectural pedants for having academic inaccuracies on the stucco Corinthian and Doric columns. Nash utilised the ornamental capacity of stucco on plain brick not just for decorative details but also to tailor and completely unify the architectural style of his buildings, the columns, parapets, walls and window surrounds. His stuccoed walls were vertically and horizontally lined to resemble courses of stone flowing from house to house then 'frescoed' to imitate the patina of weathered natural stone. Cast-iron palisade fences were painted a dark green colour to imitate aged and weathered bronze. The fanciful 'sham' of these materials and methods was, for the most part, unconsciously accepted. London did not have any local stone quarries and the use of these less expensive materials and devices was not questioned by architects until Victorian times and, with the exception of John Ruskin, more often in private than in public. Architects, then as now, were reluctant to criticise the taste of their clients.

By the 1820s, the colony in Australia was enjoying a measure of prosperity and confidence, nurtured during the time of Lachlan Macquarie's governorship.

LEFT ✦ Terrace housing in Australia was largely a middle class affair. The grandiose terraces built for the rich inhabitants of English cities, such as Carlton House Terrace, on The Mall, London, were not repeated in Australia. Begun by the architect John Nash in 1827, Carlton House Terrace is shown here being repainted in 1898. Entrance to the houses was from the back, the front being screened by a monumental row of Corinthian columns. The grandeur of such Regency and Georgian rows was often designed to be viewed from afar, as in the case of Carlton House Terrace, which has no building opposite. Terraces built on this sort of scale in parks, squares and crescents were often grander than nearby public buildings. Towns such as Bristol and Brighton also had a taste for these palatial terrace buildings.

Right (top and bottom) ◆
*Joseph Fowles thought of himself
as a marine artist, but he is
best remembered for his book,
Sydney in 1848, a collection of
copperplate engravings with
elevated views of the principal
streets of this 'Metropolis of
Australia'. He carefully
delineated the dress-circle
addresses of Sydney and
portrayed a prim town along
harmonious Georgian lines.
His keen draughting skill and
delightfully pretentious prose
have left us with a valuable
record of Sydney from which
we can trace the development
of its terraces.*

*Underwood's Tenements
(top), a terrace of shops with
residences above, situated to the
left of the offices of the* Sydney
Morning Herald, *is believed to
be Sydney's first terrace. It was
built by James Underwood
before 1826, in which year it
was depicted by a French artist
who was a member of Dumont
D'Urville's expedition that
visited Sydney that year.*

*Horbury Terrace (bottom)
in Macquarie Street was,
according to Joseph Fowles,
'the private residence of many
respectable families'. Today
there are two survivors of this
c. 1836 row of seven houses —
they can be found at 171 and
173 Macquarie Street.*

Macquarie had also improved the order and architecture of Sydney. An 1826 view of George Street[2] shows Underwood's Tenements, an undistinguished row of bald-faced houses, which was probably the first terrace

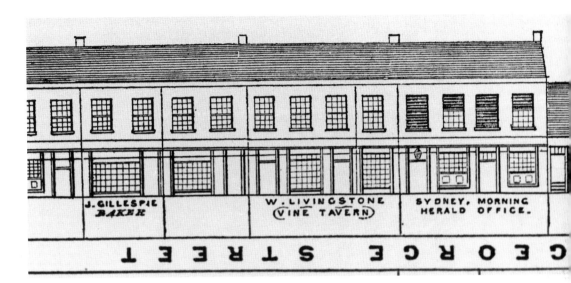

built in Australia. As the young city grew it developed the orderly aspect of a provincial English Georgian town. Terrace houses and shops, with residences above, became the norm in the centre of the city and in some surrounding towns, such as Windsor.

BELOW ◆ *Macquarie Street, Sydney, in the 1860s, was a fashionable address of the rich and well-to-do. The decorative iron balustrade on the terrace closest was thought to be fret-worked wood, but magnification shows that a heavy iron stay is supporting it. Such balustrades disappeared, probably because their weight weakened wood-framed balconies. The central house has three dainty cast-iron balconettes. The same pattern can be seen today on 171 and 173 Macquarie Street.*

From this distance in time it seems extraordinary that, when faced with a vast, new and unexplored continent, Australia's early builders were content to build houses in the style of drizzle-bound England. The invisible links with that country were strong, and most of England's urban population lived in row, or terrace, houses of one form or another. Indeed, it was free-standing houses that required a distinguishing name, such as 'cottage' or 'villa'. The use of the word 'house' usually implied a terrace house, which was the main form of rental accommodation before home-ownership became the norm. Terraces were, to put it quite simply, 'always there'. They required no separate or distinguishing name.

As the Industrial Revolution gained momentum in England, there was little distinction made between

ABOVE ◆ *The tradition of joined houses in the English countryside is repeated in early nineteenth-century farmworkers' houses at Mayfield, Tasmania. The rural mellowness belies its history as a site of conflict between early settlers and Aborigines, and of later raids by bushrangers.*

RIGHT ◆ *Windsor, a town of the Macquarie era on the outskirts of Sydney, has a Georgian character. This terrace of three houses was built with rich red bricks in 1836. The Regency-style ironwork was added later.*

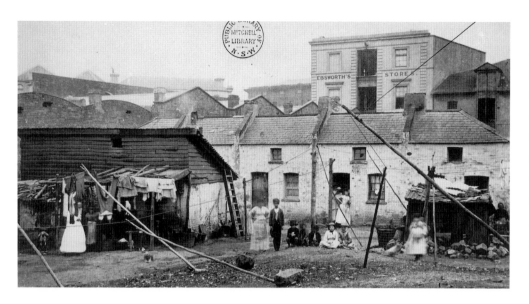

LEFT (TOP AND BOTTOM) ◆
Photographs of the houses of the rich and middle class give little indication as to how life was enjoyed, or endured, within them. These two photographs of squalid Sydney terraces, which were probably slums from the moment they were built in the 1840s, tell a fuller story. From the Mitchell Library collection, the photographs are captioned with different addresses, but strong magnification shows the houses and children to be the same. In the top picture, only the cockatoo on its perch seems to have remained motionless for the photographer. The network of clotheslines and tubs suggests the building on the left was a laundry. The blurred children in the bottom picture obviously moved, but the supremely confident cat on the crate beneath the window box of geraniums on the second house remained statue-still. Curious faces can be seen peering from the doorways of houses beyond the communal tap. The address was probably Queen's Square, which was between Pitt and George Streets, and the photos were taken in 1875, before the demolition of these appallingly cramped terraces. Terraces built during the 1880s and 1890s offered a far greater degree of space and comfort.

country and city housing. Terraces were built in tiny villages as well as in the expanding industrial cities. These distinctions overlapped to a far lesser extent in Australia, but it helps us to understand why it would not have seemed unusual to the colonists to build terraces at Windsor, 67 kilometres from Sydney, in the 1830s, or at Pontville, outside Hobart, even earlier.

The stately sweeps and crescents of the Georgian terraces of Bath and Bristol were not repeated in

Australia, but nor were the monotonous and endless rows of mean-spirited workers' terraces that are a feature of English industrial cities. Many of these abject terraces were built back-to-back, without even the benefit of a yard and an outdoor privy. A communal toilet was usually situated at the end of the row and the only water supply was a wooden barrel outside each house, fed by a downpipe from the roof.

However, echoes of both these English extremes can be discovered in Australia. French's Building in Darlinghurst and similarly appalling terrace slums in The Rocks could easily have been photographed in Dickens' London or in the north of England.

BELOW • *French's Building, an 1860s terrace in Darlinghurst, photographed in January 1871, and long since demolished. These English-style terraces were built for working-class tenants from porous-looking brick and roofed with shingles. The downpipes issued rainwater straight onto the footpath. As was common with speculative developments such as these, the last house in the row (far end) is a shop.*

The Early
Terraces of Sydney

✦✦✦

Few of the great names of early nineteenth-century Australian architecture can be linked with terrace houses, but John Verge is a notable exception. John Verge was a fashionable architect who practised in Sydney in the 1830s. Most of his commissions were for the newly rich and the landed gentry of the colony, who required elegant houses along the established lines evolved in England. He also designed terrace houses, a pair of which still stand at 39–41 Lower Fort Street in The Rocks. The Mitchell Library in Sydney has John Verge's original 1833 ink-and-wash plans for a delightful terrace of seven shops with residences above, which was built in Bridge Street. This fine Regency-style building was known as The Colonnade; its three sections stepped daintily down the hill near the intersection with George Street. It seems likely that it was painted in the elegant colours suggested in Verge's original drawing — cream with a light brown trim. The Colonnade was demolished in the latter part of the nineteenth century.

LEFT ✦ *According to his ledger for 1834, architect John Verge was paid £60 for designing and supervising the construction of this pair of terrace houses at 39–41 Lower Fort Street, The Rocks. They were auctioned in 1842. The advertisement for these fine Regency houses 'at the Sea-Breeze end of Fort Street' describes the basement as having a 'well adapted kitchen, scullery, cellars and conveniences'. The first floor 'contains a completely furnished dining room and parlour', the second included 'a capital iron balcony' and the third held three bedrooms. The coach house and stables were 'a convenient distance, avoiding . . . things not redolent to the olefactory sense'. Demolitions to make way for the southern pylons of the Sydney Harbour Bridge were to later cut a swathe through The Rocks and destroy much of its architectural character. Fortunately, this delightful terrace was overlooked.*

• *John Verge's original 1833 ink-and-wash plans for The Colonnade, held in the Mitchell Library. The terrace of seven shops with residences above was built in Bridge Street, Sydney, for speculator John Edye Manning. It had a formal, stepped colonnade more reminiscent of John Nash's London than the colonial verandahs that were to follow.*

BELOW RIGHT • *Lyons Terrace, a Regency-style terrace completed in 1841. The roofline of the building is distinguished by the raised firewalls, which were made compulsory by the Building Act passed by the Legislative Assembly of New South Wales in 1837. Other features, such as the cast-iron verandah columns and balcony panels, and the recessed alignment allowing for a front garden, were to set standards for Sydney terraces for the rest of the century. Architects and builders were to apply opulent decoration to this orderly and elegant structure with ever-increasing zest as the century progressed. But in 1848, Joseph Fowles thought these houses were 'without exception the best in the City and would not disgrace the Regent's Park in London'.*

John Verge's office ledger for February 1837 shows that he or his assistant, John Bibb, drew up plans for a terrace that was to survive into the twentieth century and was to be the prototype for the thousands of Sydney terrace houses that followed.

Lyons Terrace, in what is now Liverpool Street, opposite Hyde Park, was completed in 1841, probably under the supervision of John Bibb, as John Verge had retired from their practice two years earlier. It was built for Samuel Lyons, who, before becoming one of Sydney's most influential businessmen and builder of terraces, had a wild career as a convict. He arrived in Sydney in 1815 to serve a long sentence for theft.

LYON'S TERRACE   HYDE PARK.

He absconded several times, was recaptured and flogged. Perhaps it was his sixteen-year-old Irish bride, Mary Murphy, who was responsible for reforming him. They opened a shop after they were married in 1822 and by the time he received his full pardon in 1831 he was a wealthy auctioneer. Lyons was very proud of his row of five three-storey houses, which were said to have cost £3000 each and which were to become a fashionable address.

Lyons Terrace was a departure from the Sydney terraces built before it, and set the architectural character for most that were to follow. A new Building Act aimed at fire control came into effect in 1838,

ABOVE ✦ *Lyons Terrace set the scene for what Robin Boyd dubbed 'the Victorian ferrous adventure'. Decorative ironwork, seen here casting a filigree shadow on a Paddington balcony, produced its own folklore. The appealing (but untrue) story of iron-lace panels travelling as ships' ballast probably had its origins in the practice of ballasting ships with pig iron. Imported ironwork from England travelled as carefully packed and stowed fare-paying cargo.*

which required Lyons Terrace to have its party walls raised 1 foot 6 inches (45 centimetres) above the roofline. This gave the houses in Lyons Terrace, and all those built subsequently in Sydney, a vertical cast, with each house appearing as a 'slice' in the row. The effect is not noticeable where a high parapet hides a flat roof, but these raised party walls were to give the distinctive pattern to the rooflines of inner-city areas of Sydney that can still be seen today.

Georgian-style terraces built in Sydney prior to 1841 were built onto the street alignment, with the front door opening directly to the street. Lyons Terrace adopted the sensible feature of being set back from the street, behind an iron palisade fence, which allowed for a small front garden. Perhaps its most copied feature, and the architect's greatest bequest to Australian urban architecture (be it Verge or Bibb), was the use of repeated, covered balconies with cast-iron balustrades.

An endless row of bald-faced terrace houses as seen in bleak English industrial cities can most generously be described as wearisome. By contrast, a streetscape of double-storey terraces with repeated iron-lace balconies is stunning. The balconies, with their bold and imaginative decoration, became an enduring and distinctive feature of Australian terrace facades for the rest of the nineteenth century. ·

BELOW ✦ *Restored terraces in Glebe. Terrace houses are, by design and definition, repetitious. Australian terraces triumphed over their possible monotony by presenting to the street a perspective of lacy balconies or shaded verandahs, and a collective colour scheme that conveyed a sense of balance and harmony.*

RIGHT ✦ *Pembroke Terrace. The first six houses of Pembroke Terrace can still be found in Buckingham Street, Surry Hills. The frontages and the verandah walls of the first seven houses are built of sparrow-picked sandstone; the roofs are slate and the downpipes discharge rainwater through an open drain into the gutter. French windows and a cast-iron bootscraper can be seen on each verandah. And of course the raised firewalls, so characteristic of Sydney.*

This 1871 photograph is remarkably clear. It is possible to make out a handwritten note attached to the French windows of the third house. The upper windows are without curtains and the house appears empty, so perhaps the note says it is available for rent.

24	Bar	STREET	Bar	

Barcom Street		**Barcom Street, Little**	
From Liverpool street to Oxford street		Paddington boundary to Victoria street	
East Side			

61	Gittens, Josiah W., coppersmith
63	Sweeney, Mrs. Mary Ann
65	Mason, Joseph, undertaker
67	Sutton, Nathaniel
69	Addison, Charles, contractor
	Here Oxford street

2	Laverty, B., dairy	
	Vacant land	
6	Nicolle, Eugene D., civil engineer	
8	Vacant	
10	Power, James	
12	Goddard, Mrs.	
14	McCarty, Michael, dairy	
16	Smedley, John	
18	Stewart, Paustie, engineer	1
20	Reardon, Bernard	2
22	McCarty, Mrs.	3
24	Carroll, John, grocer	4
26	Acrit, Mrs., dressmaker	5
28	Cryen, Robert, plasterer	6
30	Crawley, Mrs. Margaret, dressmaker	7
32	Curran, Patrick, gardener	8
34	Fisher, William, painter	9
36	Barton, Henry, musician	10
38	Murray, Mrs., laundress	11
40	Morris, James, carter	12
42	Fitzpatrick, Francis, engineer	13
44	Houlahan, Mrs.	14
46	Thompson, John, carpenter	15
48	O'Grady, Edward	16
	Here Oxford street	
	West Side	

(French buildings)

Barker Lane
Barker street to Duncan street
South Side

1	Sarbier, Adam
3	Pointer, Joseph, plasterer
5	Molen, David, engineer
7	Logan, William Lloyd, clerk
9	Hughes, Frederick, enginedriver
	Walker, Robert, corkcutter
19	Brough, James, carpenter
21	Bridger, William, fruiterer
	Holmes, Henry, drayman
23	Moss, Thomas, carpenter
25	Gibson, Mrs. Maria
27	Simpson, John, engineer
	Bertleshaw, Thomas, miner
29	Reid, James, miner
	Severy, Peter
31	Snow, John, engineer
	Fox, Henry, bootmaker

LEFT AND RIGHT ✦ *These two extracts from pages 24 and 37 of the 1876 edition of Sands' New South Wales Directory show how a terrace could be its own postal address. The numbering of the individual houses within the terrace row maintain their own sequence and are quite different from their numbers as part of the street. Looking at the east side of Barcom Street, Surry Hills,*

we see that Francis Fitzpatrick, for example, lived in 13 French Building (illustrated on page 23), also known as 42 Barcom Street. Pembroke Terrace, on the west side of Buckingham Street, would appear to have had a similar social status at the time to that of French's Building, with a mix of middle-class occupants, such as commercial travellers and engineers, and working-class occupants.

Buckingham Street
Devonshire street to Cleveland street

East Side

Vacant land
6 Shortland, R.
8 Chapman, Henry W., tailor
10 Johnson, Mrs. —
12 Davies, John, blacksmith
14 Harris, William, hay and corn dealer
Vacant land
Here Rutland street
18 Stow, William, wheelwright
20 Crisford, Thomas, bootmaker
22 Rice, John, painter
24 Murray, George, carpenter
26 Manning, Henry, painter
28 Andrews, John, packer
30 Hill, John, blacksmith
34 Stone, William, letter carrier
36 Hoyle, Henry, blacksmith
38 Stewart, Robert C., clerk
40 Scott, Robert, engineer
42 Irvine, James C., warehouseman
44 Ellis, George Thomas, coachmaker
46 Halley, William, coachbuilder
48 Cobb, John, engineer
50 Hopkins, William, auctioneer
Loney, Gore W., *Czarina Arms*
Here Bedford street
Davies, John Henry, grocer
62 Nicholson, Richard, carter
64 Morris, Benjamin, draper

126 Conroy, Daniel J., jeweller
Here Cleveland street

—

West Side

17 Shortland, W. H., carrier
19 Bateup, John
21 Hetherington, Samuel, builder
23 Rigg, George, carpenter
25 Hay, Mrs.
27 Pawley, Mrs., ladies' school
29 Fisher, Thomas F., grocer
31 Doolan, Robert, engineer
33 Duckworth, Mrs. Jane
35 Tindale, William, auctioneer
37 Cooper, Mrs., fancy goods bazaar
39 Dabell, George, law clerk
41 Buckley, William, carpenter
43 Rose, Mrs., laundress
47 Anderson, John, clerk
Here Bedford street
53 Barrett & Co., ærated waters and cordial manufacturers
Vacant land
Here Belvoir street
Vacant land
99 Frost, Charles, draper
101 Pearson, W., commercial traveller
103 Thompson, Mrs. —
105 Ward, Alfred J., saddler
107 Stephen, William, engineer
109 McCloud, Donald, patternmaker
111 Thorne, John Thomas, architect

Pembroke terrace

Marvellous Melbourne

◆ ◆ ◆

Melbourne became gold-rich at the tender age of sixteen. After gold was discovered in Victoria in 1851, the city trebled its population in three years; within a decade it had increased fivefold. During the first years of the gold rush, housing was an urgent problem and the goldseekers were housed beneath shacks of canvas and stringybark or portable houses of galvanised iron that they sometimes brought with them.

As gold fortunes were made, Regency-inspired terraces were erected in streets whose names reflect the era — King William Street, Albert Street and Victoria Street.

The most impressive of these Regency terraces of the heady gold-rush era is Royal Terrace, located in Nicholson Street, Fitzroy. This elegant row of blue–grey houses was built in 1854. It is perhaps the most visually satisfying Australian terrace of its era. The orderly rhythm of its windows and its striped, concave verandah roofs give it the dignified mood and character of this period.

ABOVE ◆ *Royal Terrace, a fine terrace that evoked the early mood of the gold-rush Regency style, in Nicholson Street, Fitzroy. This lithographic view is from Charles Troedel's book,* The Melbourne Album, *published in 1863. It was built in 1854, and the design has been attributed to the architect John Gill.*

Dignity, however, was not necessarily what gold-rich Melbourne was seeking. The symmetry and restraint of the colonial Georgian mansions of Sydney were considered desperately boring — a stern military architecture built during a shameful convict past. The mood of Melbourne was quickly becoming one of confidence and prosperity and it wanted a city that reflected that spirit of opulence and grandeur. Nor did the slightly more ornate Regency style offer enough opportunity for self-advertisement, or properly represent the high self-esteem of 'marvellous Melbourne'. Modesty was as unknown to Melbourne's architects of the time as it was to its journalists, who coined such descriptions of their city. But the wealth-generated architecture that its architects created was to give Melbourne buildings of great distinction.

Melbourne's streets, unlike those of Sydney, which followed the meandering bullock tracks of the early convict settlement, were wide and leafy and laid out in a grid pattern, similar in design to the *colonia* of the iron-willed Romans. Churches were prominently situated opposite a court house or a monumental government building, with an imposing statue of

ABOVE ✦ *Royal Terrace. This row of almost identical, finely detailed bluestone houses is one of the most impressive terraces in Melbourne. Today, sparklingly restored, it retains its original air of dignified understatement.*

ABOVE ✦ *Melbourne's single-storey terraces often wear high parapets to carry a full display of decoration to allay any hint of plainness. This house at 75 Keppel Street, Carlton, declares its loyalty to Empire and to the Italianate with the Imperial crown set in its Classical entablature.*

Queen Victoria (instead of Caesar) overlooking the square between. The elegant crescents and terraced circular 'squares' that featured in the speculative housing developments of Regency and Victorian London were rarely built in Melbourne.

The full impact of the era of Queen Victoria commenced in the 1860s, when Melbourne became the centre of Australian prosperity, growth and architectural fashion. Melbourne's public and private buildings were dressed in all the exotic and disputing styles of Europe. Banks and public buildings pro-claimed their status with fluted Corinthian columns and Classical porticos or, if they leant to the Gothic, with medieval spires, towers and battlements. Town halls flaunted their independence with Italianate clock towers, 'visible proof', according to the *Argus*, 'of the success and popularity of self government'.

During the 1860s and 1870s the character of Australian terrace houses developed into the form that is so recognisable today. Two-storey houses wore a dainty balcony with a cast-iron balustrade of a simple pattern, of more void than fill, and still quite staid when compared to the ostentatious 'ferromania' that was to follow. Parapet design and ornamentation were also understated compared to that of the following decades; the central house usually wore a Classical triangular pediment with an entablature bearing the name of the row, such as Belgravia Terrace or Canterbury Terrace. These can still be seen on some semi-detached houses, which would also have been dubbed 'terraces'.

The terraces built in Australia from this period onwards ranged from one storey to five storeys in height and had frontages from the minuscule, about 3 metres wide, up to the grandiose, with a width of over 10 metres. All, how-ever, had one feature in common, which deter-mined the interior plan of the main part of the house: unless a house was at the end of a row, on a street corner, it could not have

BELOW • 12 Commonwealth Street (formerly Macquarie Street), Surry Hills, an example of the minuscule as opposed to the grandiose. This 1870s terrace house had a frontage only two and a half times the width of its front door, or about 2.1 metres. It featured a twelve-pane, double-hung window and a handsome four-panel door with prominent bolection, or moulding. The gas lamp standard on the street bears an Australian Foundry casting mark. These houses were demolished in 1903.

RIGHT ✦ *An elegant, wide-balconied 1870s terrace in St Vincent Place — lacy white prettiness, Victorian rectitude, and a sense of wellbeing.*

St Vincent Place, in Albert Park, was laid out in 1857. It is one of Melbourne's rare London-style rectangular 'squares', with its terraces and houses overlooking a landscaped and leafy park.

windows along its two side walls. These walls were, of course, party walls, shared with the neighbouring houses on either side. A terrace house could therefore only be two rooms deep, as a middle room would have no access to a window. This problem was overcome by having those rooms that extended beyond the basic two built on a narrower width, thus creating a type of alleyway between the inner side walls and allowing windows to be built into those walls. The term 'tunnel-back' was applied to this light-well, formed where the narrower walls did not occupy the full width of the house. This system provided a source of light to the upper storeys as well as to the ground level. Three-storey terraces are quite common in both Melbourne and Sydney. One of the landmarks of the latter city is a four-storey terrace in King's Cross called Brent Terrace, which was built in the 1890s.

Melbourne entered a phenomenal period of urban growth during the 1880s, which altered every aspect of the city's life. A speculative mentality developed, with a taste for unrestrained and ostentatious display. Nothing reflected Melbourne's vision of itself more than its exuberant domestic and public architecture. Subdivided land was often bought and sold a number

of times within a short period before it was finally
built upon. Most of the extravagant terrace houses we
see today were built during times of aggressive prosperity and pride. Terrace houses of the boom years
were the equivalent of today's 'flats' — they were
built by speculators primarily to provide rental
accommodation. Many of the builders, however, chose
to live in them, usually in the central house in the row,
which often had a few extra flourishes of decoration.

LEFT ◆ *Rochester Terrace is another of the terraces of St Vincent Place. It has ten houses, all of mansion-sized proportions, but its lush garden makes it impossible to photograph as a single entity. The end house pictured here finishes the row with an elaborate flourish. Its columns have echoes of Nash's London.*

Antiquity
Invades the Antipodes

Seldom has domestic architecture ever adopted so many exotic styles and delighted in such a variety of ornament. Whether building mansions at St Kilda or row housing at Carlton, builders, designers and architects looked only backwards for inspiration. Innovation was apparent only in the ways in which elements as disparate as Gothic, Classical, French Chateau, Scottish Baronial and Italianate styles and types of ornamentation were combined.

There was no shortage of pattern books available at the time that depicted the emblems and motifs of antiquity and the Middle Ages. Parapets were heavily encrusted with Roman swags, garlands and festoons, and plaster urns and Classical busts sat upon their pediments. Parapets themselves grew higher to accommodate their load of ornament; on a single-storey house, a parapet was almost as high as the house it was mounted upon. Precast grotesque faces and masks stared out over the street from the narrow ends of dividing walls. The rest of the wall could be incised

RIGHT ✦ The anonymous rhymster who bemused London with the following ditty refers to John Nash and his lavish use of stucco (then known as plaster), in lieu of carved stone, to model architectural features on his Regency-style buildings. He also made use of cast iron. Stucco and ironwork were eventually to become synonymous with Victorian-era architecture.

'Augustus at Rome was for building renowned and of marble he left, what of brick he had found. But is not our Nash, too, a very great master? He finds us all brick and leaves us all plaster.'

These terraces at 168 and 170 Gatehouse Street, Parkville, in Melbourne, give an indication of how the use of cast iron and stucco translated from England to the Antipodes. Both houses have the distinctive Melbourne features of round columns and wooden handrails.

37

BELOW ✦ *Victorians loved clutter inside their houses as well as on the facades outside. Pictures and plates adorn the walls of this 1890s parlour in Balmain, Sydney. Books and vases cover the desk and table, and there are lyrebird tail feathers among the urns, vases and curios on the mantlepiece. The walls are papered and the lights are gasoliers.*

with designs in the render or lined to imitate ashlar. Other areas were coated with stucco, which was incised while still wet with sinuous vine leaves and mouldings — all this to avoid the Victorian horror of a blank wall. The earlier uncluttered patterns on cast-iron balcony panels were discarded and foundries produced an astounding range of designs embodying Gothic, Classical and Renaissance motifs, usually combined with a floral pattern.

Antiquity invaded the antipodes. A stuccoed head of a bearded Hercules, wearing his traditional lion's pelt helmet, watched blindly from terrace house walls. Flora, the Roman goddess of spring, cast in iron and delicately painted, skittered across balcony railings strewing flowers before her. Cupids aimed their arrows from cast-iron balcony panels.

When not imitating the past, some foundry pattern makers and etched glass designers of the time occasionally turned to the Australian bush for inspiration. The flannel flower and bush ferns appeared in decorative panels of both cast iron and etched glass, along with kookaburras, sulphur-crested cockatoos and the wattlebird.

Other designs were stridently imperialistic. The crown and the floral emblems of the British Isles, the rose, shamrock and thistle, were themes commonly found throughout this period, known for its pride in and celebration of a pompous and belligerent British Empire.

The incongruities and contradictions of Victorian-era architecture and its cosmetics must be linked with a British nationalism that seems completely alien to most Australians today. Britain was still thought of as 'home' by many Australians, and loyalty to the dour and dumpy queen knew no bounds.

Prior to the centenary year of 1888, a Brisbane foundry, H. Sargeant and Co., designed and registered for copyright a commemorative Australian cast iron balcony panel. This featured a kangaroo and emu beneath an Australian tree fern, flanked by a series of other panels of spear-wielding, but modestly girded,

ABOVE ✦ *Flora, the Roman goddess of spring, captured in cast iron and delicate hues on a balcony.*

Aboriginal hunters. A matching bracket also featured kangaroos and emus in a type of Australian coat of arms, surrounded by a tendril nostalgically sprouting a rose, shamrock and thistle. Such national sentiment was drowned out in the rampant imperialist jingoism of the centenary year, and today, this design is noted for its rarity. The shamrock, however, was to remain ubiquitous, especially in New South Wales, where it is often seen with the Harp of Erin.

LEFT ✦ *A bracket featuring English, Irish, Scottish and Australian symbols. This was a Queensland design produced during the centennial year of 1888.*

BELOW ✦ *A clear case of Irish nationalism on a Glebe balcony. These Harp of Erin panels are in fact beautifully cast and maintained aluminium reproductions, so defiantly accurate that a magnet is needed to determine whether they are cast-iron originals. Faithful aluminium reproductions such as these have a weight advantage when used on a cantilevered balcony. Shabby imitations are immediately identifiable as pseudo-antique.*

Abstraction Abandonment

❖❖❖

The thirst for novelty and profusion in domestic decoration continued throughout the economic and urban boom of the 1880s. But what were the people of this era trying to convey with this excess? A respect for the heraldry of the past, or a pride in their economic progress, change and innovation?

Probably the latter. The visual exuberance of the terrace facades sought to shed lustre on the owner's prosperity and social status. As a fashion that relied on the implied prosperity of the time, high Victorianism reached its climax at the point of economic collapse. In 1892 Melbourne's economic bubble burst amidst sensational scandals of corruption and embezzlement

RIGHT ✦ The colours of the Australian terraces were often surprisingly subdued, especially when compared with the extraordinary opulence of their ornamentation. The original contrasting browns can still be seen on this terrace pediment in Surry Hills, Sydney.

ABOVE ✦ This c. 1870 working-class terrace on the corner of O'Connor and Balfour Streets, Chippendale, was photographed in about 1910. Lighting for the street and the houses would have been by gas — note the pipes entering the houses beside the windows. The chimneys indicate

coal fires were used for heating purposes. The tops of the party walls and the end wall are render-sealed to protect against damp, and the frontages are of unpainted brick on a sandstone base-course. The photographer provides entertainment for the children and the woman above.

involving some of Melbourne's most prominent politicians and businessmen.

Banks closed their doors and a harrowing economic depression followed. Building abruptly stopped in Melbourne and, to a lesser extent, in Sydney, and did not fully recover until the new century. Prosperity had literally gone west, in this instance to Perth, where gold discoveries were doing for Perth what they had done for Melbourne forty years earlier.

ABOVE ◆ *Although no longer the dominant architectural style for housing, terraces were still built in the twentieth century. Ornate woodwork replaced iron on this Federation terrace in Cascade Street, Paddington, but some Victorian elements, such as stucco consoles and cast cement urns, overlapped into this era.*

The new century ushered in a new style of domestic architecture — what we now refer to as 'Federation' architecture. Australians found the casual space and amplitude of this new style to their liking, believing that it was appropriate to their new nation and the new century. They broke free of the confined notions of the nineteenth century and quickly adapted to the concept of suburban living in a free-standing, single-storey house connected to the city via an improved rail or tram service.

Victorian formality gave way to a new, casual nonchalance. A red brick house with terracotta roof tiles, surrounded by a garden behind a timber picket fence, now represented middle-class values and family comfort. However, some speculative building of terraces continued well into the twentieth century. These terraces were usually adorned with the symbols of the Federation era; occasionally, they had dainty Art Nouveau designs on their balcony panels. As always, there were exceptions — a row of Victorian-style

terraces in Lithgow, New South Wales, bears the date 1919, and one in Forbes Street, Woolloomooloo, 1931.

For most Australians, however, terraces heaped with effusive Victorian ornamentation became a dishonoured and disgraced style — perhaps as a result of confusing ornament with design. Australian cities were suddenly ashamed of their older terrace houses. The middle classes abandoned them, and the terrace areas of the inner city were inhabited only by those who could not afford to move out into the suburbs.

ABOVE ✦ *An Art Nouveau cast-iron pattern on the balcony of a twentieth-century terrace house in Carlton, Melbourne.*

ABOVE ✦ *Westgate Terrace, in Ruthven Street, Bondi Junction, presents an irregular and broken facade to the street. Traces of the original rich cream and Venetian-red colour scheme can still be seen on the parapet.*

RIGHT ✦ *Cast-iron decoration crossed all class barriers. The same design seen on this unprepossessing terrace at Bondi Junction (photographed c. 1905) could be found on the city mansions of the rich, on grandiose homesteads and on country pub verandahs. The cast-iron panels that were used were likely to be the result of an arbitrary choice made by the builder from a foundry catalogue. Individual or customised castings were extremely rare (see page 91 for one example).*

Paint peeled from the richly stuccoed walls and parapets, giving the terraces an air of mouldering seediness. Balconies lost their grace and delicacy as they sagged under the weight of rusting iron or were enclosed to serve as additional, rickety bedrooms. The facades, designed for eye-catching display and showy self-advertisement, looked even sadder and more dishonoured in their neglect. They were to wait half a century for rehabilitation.

ABOVE ✦ *This arcaded terrace of seven houses in Erskineville, Sydney, is of a distinctly Melbourne style. Photographed in 1936, with the effects of the Depression still being felt, the houses have taken on an air of faded and shabby gentility. From the nuances of black and white, however, it appears that their Victorian colour scheme is still intact. This building has since been demolished.*

NOTES

1. Robert Adam, in his *Works in Architecture*, 1778, describes his illustration of the Adelphi Terrace as follows: 'The above print exhibits the Royal Terras, the Houses and Openings of the streets leading to the Strand'.
2. See R. Irving, *The History and Design of the Australian House*, 1985, p. 23.

47

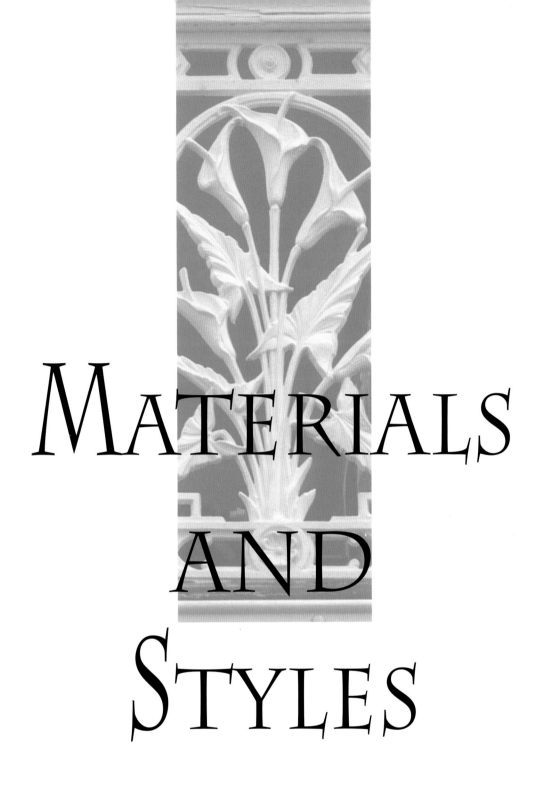

MATERIALS AND STYLES

... even the less pretentious structures bear many marks of taste, and an advanced state of embellishment.

J. INGLIS, *OUR AUSTRALIAN COUSINS*, 1880

The Shades and Nuances of a City

◆◆◆

PREVIOUS PAGE ◆ A free-standing nineteenth-century house at 69 Kerferd Road, Albert Park, Melbourne. Its alternating courses of cream, red and black bricks give it a strong individual character.

Sydney had the good fortune to be founded on a great bed of honey-coloured sandstone. The city that rose above this rock strata took on the same golden colour as the stone from its quarries. The sandstone character of Sydney lasted throughout the nineteenth century; it was used for housing, public buildings, warehouses and even street kerbing and guttering.

LEFT ◆ Catherine Terrace. The c. 1870 sandstone-fronted houses at 11–17 Stanley Street, Darlinghurst, are plain save for the ironwork on their balconies.

50

ABOVE ◆ *Sandstone Sydney.
Carlton Terrace in York Street,
Sydney, photographed in 1870.
The massive Classical verandah
columns are Ionic and are cast*
*iron; those on the balconies are of
the same material, cast in a simple
flat grille pattern. The house on
the right is not part of the terrace;
its alignment on the footpath is*
*more advanced. It also has four
storeys whereas Carlton Terrace
has a basement level. The house
at the far end has an observatory.
The corner wall shows that sand-*
*stone was used only as the facade.
The walls are of brick and laid in
an English bond, one course laid
lengthways (stretchers), the next
laid end-on (headers).*

The first stone to be used was laboriously prised from outcrops on the western side of Sydney Cove, known as 'The Rocks'. The first government quarry helped level the area that is now Argyle Place. The clay beneath the southern end of Sydney was used to make early sandstock bricks — highly porous, but beautifully coloured in saffron yellows and apricot–pinks speckled with purple and black. Bricks were being moulded within three months of the arrival of the First Fleet. Brick and stone have always remained the favoured building materials of this city. Sandstone, sometimes known as 'freestone', was used either dressed or 'sparrow picked', and bricks became cheaper and of better quality when coal discoveries allowed the brick kilns to be fired by coal instead of wood.

Australian timbers were to receive a bad press from the first builders at Sydney Cove. Above the strata of sandstone were forests of *Angophora costata*, or Sydney red gum, probably the most 'useless' of Australian timbers. The convicts broke and blunted their tools on its trunks, and the irregular timber warped and cracked soon after it was cut. Before stringybark and ironbark

RIGHT ✦ An 1840s terrace of minuscule sandstone houses in McElhone Street, Surry Hills. It is thought that these tiny houses were built to accommodate the families of soldiers stationed at nearby Victoria Barracks.

were discovered, the disgruntled builders thought the local timber was fit only for burning. 'I do not know for any one purpose for which it will answer', wrote First Fleet surgeon John White in 1790, 'except for firewood; and for that it is excellent'.

BELOW ✦ *Melbourne's architects and builders took advantage of the local cobalt, rich cream and ochre bricks to create multi-coloured patterns on walls, chimneys and window surrounds with skilfully laid brickwork. Here it adds zest to the wall of an end terrace in St Vincent Place, Albert Park.*

When stands of Australian cedar were later discovered in the forests of the north coast of New South Wales, the timber quickly became a popular building material. In *Sydney in 1848* Joseph Fowles speaks proudly of staircases 'finely wrought in Australian cedar' and fireplace surrounds 'of Colonial marble'.

Hobart and Melbourne also took on the hues and textures of their native stone — Hobart, a golden brown sandstone, and Melbourne, the smoky grey of its intractable basalt, which became known as 'bluestone'. In Adelaide, slabs of brownish-tinged grey slate were also called 'bluestone' and they were used for walling, while window surrounds and quoins were usually in brick.

There is a far greater variety of clays in the Melbourne region, which yielded up brilliant rose, yellow and cream bricks. These were used to great effect, the polychrome brickwork being found in chimneys, window surrounds and quoins. In Sydney, bricks were often covered with a skin of stucco and either lined to imitate stone or moulded into architectural features. The more elaborate stucco-work in Melbourne was less often painted.

A number of stucco patents, such as Parker's Roman Cement, had been used on London terraces as early as the 1780s. The

RIGHT ◆ *The three-storey Holcombe Terrace located at 215–219 Drummond Street, Carlton, shown here while undergoing restoration. It is built of cream and blue–grey bricks, which are sometimes called 'Hawthorn blacks' and resemble the colour of Melbourne bluestone.*

English architect John Nash used a skin of stucco, lined and grooved, as a *trompe l'oeil*, a cheaper imitation of stone, which was expensive because there were no stone quarries close to the London area. This usage became more popular after Waterloo and prompted the anonymous ditty on page 37. Nash was later to exploit the ornamental qualities of stucco to create the overall architectural style of a building — the pilasters, pediments and pillared porticoes. These were then 'frescoed' to give the appearance of weathered stone.

The elaborate stucco decoration in Melbourne has passed the harshest test of them all — time. Today it remains crisp, firm and unweathered, even where the bricks and mortar supporting it have powdered and crumbled. It is said that many Italian craftsmen were brought to Melbourne during the building boom of the 1880s and that it is they who were responsible for the high quality of that city's stucco mouldings.

Not all terraces were built of stone or brick. Some were built of weatherboard (see opposite), but few have survived. Colonial houses were roofed with wooden shingles until mid-Victorian times, when imported English slate became the prestige roofing material. However, behind the raised parapet of many a terrace

ABOVE ✦ *Lush Victoriana expressed in iron and stucco along Canning Street, North Melbourne. The shell motif seen here on the fence pillars has its roots in antiquity, and was later employed as the emblem of medieval pilgrimage. It was revived again by the designers of the Victorian era.*

house, where the flat skillion roof could not be seen, galvanised iron was invariably used. By the 1880s, corrugated, galvanised-iron roofs were a familiar sight in all Australian cities, and today it is hard to imagine an Australian country town without it. It was lightweight, transportable and had the additional bonus of being an efficient catchment for rain water for drinking. In Broken Hill, entire houses and terraces were constructed with corrugated iron and are still referred to as 'tinnies'.

BELOW ◆ *Weatherboard and iron rows have all but vanished. This one, which once stood at the corner of Hart and Elizabeth Streets, in Surry Hills, was photographed before its 1913 demolition. The photographer is a source of much curiosity on the part of the residents, children and adults alike.*

Regional Differences

The story of the Australian terrace house is not simply a tale of two cities, Sydney and Melbourne. Terraces were built in Adelaide, Brisbane, Launceston, Fremantle and Perth, as well as large country centres such as Albury, Bathurst, Ballarat and Goulburn.

BELOW LEFT • *With a tropical climate and abundant timber, Queenslanders preferred free-standing timber dwellings. However, brick terraces such as 19–25 Wellington Street, Petrie-Terrace, were built in Brisbane during the boom period. Built by speculator John O'Keefe, neither he nor subsequent owners lived there. Records show the early tenants had working-class occupations: dressmaker, fireman and railway employee.*

BELOW • *Gogg's Terrace, Ipswich, in a 1936 photo, is an unusual design of five houses flanking a carriageway. It is an example of northern-hemisphere design introduced with no concessions to the new climate except for some blinds.*

There are strong regional differences between the terraces that were built in the Australian State capitals. Melbourne terraces, both single and double storey, carry higher and more ornate parapets than those of Sydney, which usually have skillion roofs behind them. The parapet's height is often not in proportion to the height of the house upon which it stands; however, this accentuated height does stress the overall horizontal unity of the row. A Sydney terrace house is more likely to have a pitched roof, visible from the street, with a projected party wall that rises above the roof and often projects at the front of

ABOVE ✦ *Shaded by a peppercorn tree, this terrace of four sandstone houses can be found in the main street of Wilcannia, on the banks of the Darling River, in outback New South Wales. Possibly, the houses were used as shipping offices during the 1880s and 1890s, when Wilcannia was a major inland port for the riverboat trade.*

LEFT • *Sydney terraces: pitched roofs and projected party walls.*

RIGHT • *This delightful c. 1910 photograph of houses in Regent Street, Redfern, provides a concise illustrated guide to the progression of Sydney terraces. If the building on the right was shorn of its verandah, it could be any pair of Georgian terrace shops in Joseph Fowles' Sydney in 1848. Number 23, next door, is colonial Regency and may date from the 1850s. The cast-iron panels on its open balcony seek to imitate wrought iron and the pattern is one of the oldest to be seen in Sydney. The tallest house, in the centre, probably dates from the late 1860s, when uncovered balconies were still common. The ironwork is of a florid French pattern and the rendered wall at street level is lined and moulded to resemble rusticated masonry. The two terrace houses on the left are emblazoned with all the architectural symbols of the boom period of the late 1880s. The circular headed windows and the three-panel door are topped with moulded hoods and the pre-cast urns on the parapet show no signs of ageing. The flat grille columns are a feature of Sydney, rarely seen elsewhere. The sign in the window of the last house reads 'Rooms for Let'.*

each house to divide the verandahs and balconies. This asserts the vertical segmentation, or 'separateness', of each house without disturbing the visual unity of the row. All terrace houses, of course, have party walls; they are a constructional necessity. However, terraces that are visually dominated by the party wall are more common in Sydney, while the parapet type of terrace predominates in Melbourne, though both types can be seen in either city.

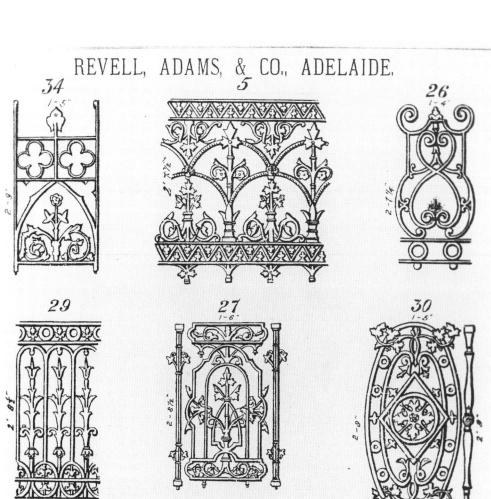

REVELL, ADAMS, & CO., ADELAIDE.

TOP LEFT ✦ *The real and the imitation vie for attention on a Paddington balcony.*

LEFT AND RIGHT ✦ *In the nineteenth century, ironwork was mass-produced by foundries and then sold to builders and architects via illustrated catalogues. These pages are from the 1886 edition of* Vulcan Iron Works Pattern Book, *the catalogue of Revell Adams and Co., Gouger Street, Adelaide.*

'Iron lace' is in fact a twentieth-century term. This nineteenth-century foundry catalogue refers to it as both 'balcony railings' (left) and 'garden railings' (right). The panel marked 29 is a distinctive Adelaide pattern not seen elsewhere. Patterns 30 and 34 are rarely found today. Possibly, few panels survived because of their fragile design. The panels cost 8 shillings each and their matching posts, 2 shillings.

ABOVE ✦ There was no class distinction in the use of decorative ironwork. The pattern of sunflowers in a vase on this free-standing Victorian mansion at 52 Powlett Street, East Melbourne, can be found on other, more modestly sized terraces throughout that city.

Melbourne balconies usually have a bulky wooden handrail along the top of the cast-iron balustrades; Sydney's are topped with a thin iron one. Melbourne decoration in iron and stucco is more lavish and exuberant. Deep aprons of ironwork hang in curving arches below the balconies, often with matching elements in the fringe, balusters and brackets. The opulent ornamentation and arched brackets on the houses illustrated on page 63 are quintessentially Melburnian and rarely seen in Sydney. Equally, the flat grille columns sighted so often on the balconies of Sydney terraces are seldom seen in Melbourne (see the shop pictured on page 84).

Adelaide's discreet bluestone terraces do not wear the extravagant and excessive ornament of the eastern cities. Ironwork is usually limited to brackets and fringes. The fences of North Adelaide's terrace houses have the distinctive, engaging characteristic of open cast-iron panels mounted on low brick walls.

There are pockets of terrace houses in Fremantle and Perth. In Catherine Street, Subiaco, there is a delightful terrace of eleven houses built in 1904, which is distinguished by the emblem of Western Australia, the black swan, moulded in stucco on the pediment of the central house.

ABOVE ◆ *This beautifully restored terrace in Subiaco, Perth, is chauvinistically Western Australian. It carries the State symbol, the black swan, on its pediment. The balusters with the palmette pattern were probably imported from Adelaide.*

Another unusual example, and certainly an unexpected sight to be found in a country town, is the cramped row of sandstone terrace houses in the wide, usually empty, main street of Wilcannia, in outback New South Wales (see page 59). And Bowen Terrace, a row of fourteen double-storey houses built in 1876, can be found in Orange, in the central west of New South Wales. Its verandah and balcony are deep and shady, in the style of a country pub, well suited to the hotter inland climate. Like many rows of terraces in Sydney, the numbers of its houses run 11, 12A, 15 — there is no unlucky 13.

Battle of the Styles

◆◆◆

The nineteenth century is remembered for its 'revivals' and 'neos'. The architecture of the Victorian era was dominated by the rival styles of the Gothic and the Classical Revivalists, and was strangely out of step with the phenomenal progress that was being made in science, industrialisation and engineering at the time. The mood and atmosphere of Victorianism was one of great abundance and sumptuousness; its enemy was anything plain. For this reason, the Victorians found the architecture of the recent past unappealing. The symmetry of the plain Georgian surfaces was thought to be boring, and neither did the more Classical Regency style please. There was also a prodigious appetite for picturesque and antiquarian fantasy. Designers of this period were able to create a railway steam engine for which there was no tradition, no precursor to draw upon, but architects wished only to exalt the distant past. The new steel bridge or railway tunnel, a miracle of engineering at the time, was likely to have pylons or a portal in imitation of a Roman triumphal arch.

The Victorian values of moral earnestness, rectitude and national pride, and a strong assertion of

LEFT • *Botanic Chambers, a terrace of seven houses built in 1877 in North Terrace, is an Adelaide landmark. It was built in conjunction with the Botanic Club House, now the Botanic Hotel, which can be seen at the end of the row. It was designed by architect Michael McMullen with Italianate-style features such as the keystone motifs on the arches of the faceted bay windows and moulded arches above the upper windows.*

N HARROW, MIDDLESEX.——MR. T. HARRIS, ARCHITECT.

Christianity, were gratified by the architecture of the Gothic Revivalists, who wished to establish it as Britain's national style. Classicism was also used freely and with a flourish, though the Goths hinted darkly at its 'pagan' origins in Ancient Greece and Rome. If religious, a building had to be Gothic; if administrative, a gaol or court house for example, it was intimidatingly and sternly Classical.

The Classical and its substyles gradually gained the ascendant position in the 'Battle of the Styles'

ABOVE ◆ *The 'castellated' style in Paddington. Battle axes and crenellations decorate Warwick, a terrace on the corner of Windsor and Cascade Streets.*

LEFT ◆ *This design for a terrace in Harrow, Middlesex, by English architect Thomas Harris, appeared in* The Builder *in October 1860. It shows that the possibilities for Gothic gloom and pretentiousness knew no bounds. This terrace was, perhaps fortunately, never built.*

ABOVE ✦ *This 1870s terrace in Forbes Street, Woolloomooloo, has overtones of the peaky Gothic style — steep gables with traceried barges, tall chimneys and an ecclesiastic design in the ironwork on its balconies.*

(as this nineteenth-century architectural dilemma has come to be known), while the Italianate style slowly came to replace post-Regency influences in Australian terraces. The Italianate is not identifiable by any one feature but draws on a whole repertoire of Renaissance elements; quoining, the arch with a keystone motif, console brackets and, in particular, the moulded, semi-circular window hood. An Italianate mansion or public building proclaimed its importance with a tower; on a terrace house, a tower was reduced to a remnant, to survive as a faceted bay window.

Many architects argued for the Italianate on the grounds that its sunny Mediterranean precedents were much more suited to the Australian climate than were

RIGHT ✦ *Free-standing houses in the terrace style were sometimes built on large blocks of land, with windows along their side walls. And despite the implied contradictions, the term 'free-standing terrace' seems to be entering the vocabulary. This Italianate-style house is just such a terrace, at 43 Park Drive, Parkville, Melbourne.*

gloomy Gothic spires. The Goths denounced the Italianate as unpatriotic and unChristian. Australian terraces did not participate fully in the Battle of the Styles, though the occasional Gothic banner was flown; some peaky Sydney terraces have steep gables, chimney clusters and ecclesiastic designs on the ironwork. Most leaned towards the Italianate and the Classical. Melbourne has the best examples of the Classical, to be seen in Clarendon Terrace in East Melbourne (page 14) and Rochester Terrace in St Vincent Place (page 36).

Most builders of terraces followed few rules when it came to the issue of style. They were too preoccupied by the pursuit of novelty and chose elements eclectically. The result is known as 'Boom style'. Except in more grandiose terraces, the repetitive nature of a run of terraces was not suited to the formal structures of Gothic spires or Italianate towers, which were more effective when used to distinguish and to declare the style of a free-standing house. Instead, a hectic mix of the heraldry and motifs of each and every style was applied to terraces — in stucco, cast cement and iron — with great bravado. 'Boom

RIGHT ◆ *Terraces built as one were usually painted as one. This terrace in Mitchell Street, Glebe, wears a uniform of traditional colours that asserts its unity and cohesion.*

style' is an entirely apt description for the heady mix of optimism and extravagance that characterised this period of Australian architecture. And terrace houses are the quintessence of that mood of nineteenth-century urban Australia.

TODAY'S RESPLENDENT VICTORIANS

A wealthy community always erects decorated buildings.

DR CHRISTOPHER DRESSER, *STUDIES IN DESIGN*, 1876

Everything old is new again.

PETER ALLEN AND CAROLE BAYER-SAGER, 'ALL THAT JAZZ', 1979

Neos and Now

◆◆◆

Today the 'neos' of Australian nineteenth-century architecture are new again; the 'revivals' are well and truly revived. The outrageous and delightful excesses of boom-style terraces have been restored, often in the colours of the Victorian-era palette and, behind their century-old facades, many have been renovated for modern living. So now, to compound the confusions of Victorian architectural jargon and its quest to revive

ABOVE • *Ballarat Terrace, a beautifully proportioned terrace at 227–231 Lydiard Street North, Ballarat. It was designed in 1889 by local architects, James and Piper, for publican Hugh Raverty. The elegant frontage is spoilt only by the telegraph pole.*

the architectural fashions of the past, we have a 'Victorian Revival' — or revivalism revived.

Every age has used the heraldry and mythology of the past to promote itself, and in doing so, keeps the cycle of fashion turning. Vitruvius, a Roman architect at the time of Christ, was scathing about the use of fanciful mythological ornament and fresco painting on the walls of Roman villas. He wrote in Book 3 of his *Ten Books on Architecture*:

> actual realities are scorned in these days of bad taste ... For instance, reeds are put in the place of columns, fluted appendages with curly leaves and volutes, instead of pediments, candelabra supporting representatives of shrines, and on top of their pediments ... having human faces seated upon them ... others with the heads of animals.

The rediscovery of Roman decoration in the late fifteenth century made a tremendous imaginative impact on design and ornament. This was heightened during the late eighteenth century, when many artists flocked to the excavation of Pompeii to make copies of the Roman domestic wall paintings that had so upset Vitruvius. Antique ornament became so much a part of the cycle of decorative fashion that its ancient origins were unknown to many of those Victorian designers who used it.

Almost 2000 years after Vitruvius, Charles L. Kingslake, an arbiter of Victorian domestic design, noted the influence. He complained in his 1868 book, *Hints on Household Taste*, about both the degree and type of ornamentation used on London shopfronts:

BELOW ◆ *The grotesque mask repeated on this fallen architrave, which forms part of a Roman theatre lying in the ruins of Side, in Turkey, was revived and found a place as domestic ornament during the Victorian era.*

LEFT ◆ *Victorian architectural and sartorial finery pose proudly for the camera at Summerfield Terrace, 40 Porter Street, Waverley, in Sydney, 1898.*

The engraved stucco designs on the projected firewalls have been delicately picked out and emphasise the separateness of these Italianate terrace houses. The elaborately moulded chimney resembles a tower and the massive wooden fenceposts have decorative heads. The iron-lace balcony remains only as a feature, as it has been enclosed with a sliding glass window. Small details in the ironwork have been picked out separately. The only thing that appears to be missing is the cast-iron 'drop' from the centre of the iron fringe under the verandah, though it is present on the balcony. This house is still standing, and is currently undergoing restoration.

'loading ... upper stories with pediments, columns, niches and cornices, just as if they stood on a basement as solid as that of the Pitti Palace'.

Perhaps the unknown writer of Ecclesiastes has defined this phenomenon even more succinctly: 'There is nothing new under the sun.'

As domestic architectural fashions swung in fifty-year sweeps of the pendulum, so too did the social status and the prestige of inner-city suburbs, which have undergone the most startling reversals and changes throughout the twentieth century.

Protective Neglect

— ✦✦✦ —

At the end of the first chapter, we left the terrace house areas being abandoned in droves by the middle classes, who sought the leafy quietude of the new Federation-style suburbs at the turn of the century. Thousands of inner-city terraces, laden with confections of suddenly outdated decoration, mouldered into decrepitude. Formerly fashionable addresses, such as St Vincent Place, Melbourne — a beautifully laid out square of terraces and mansions — and Sydney's Paddington — a stolid, middle-class terrace suburb —

BELOW ∙ *A terrace of outside loos. They stand sentry-like in their backyards, in a fresh coat of paint, sensibly retained for use as storage space.*

ABOVE ◆ *These Surry Hills children have stopped their cart races to watch the photographer take this pre-demolition picture of 73–77 Foveaux Street in 1909. Despite their abandonment, the paintwork on the houses still has the freshness of an earlier, Victorian era, made clear from the varying shades of grey. The box on the cart on the left is labelled 'Guinness Stout', shipped from 'J. Burke, Dublin'.*

fell into disrepute. The back alleys of Carlton, now a trendy terrace suburb, were called 'the narrows' during the 1920s, the heady underworld days of prostitution, illegal betting and race-fixing. It was there that Melbourne's urban Ned Kelly, the gangster 'Squizzy' Taylor, was shot dead in a blazing gun battle in 1927.

The roomy double-storey terrace houses were mostly turned into 'residentials'. Balconies were enclosed and larger bedrooms were divided and let to lodgers. In the 1930s, to be living in 'a room, in a reso, in Paddo' meant that a person had hit rock bottom and was really down on his or her luck in Depression-era Sydney.

LEFT ✦ *Cheswold, a concertina terrace house in Jersey Road, Paddington. 'Concertina' terraces are staggered at an angle to, as opposed to running parallel with, the street, so that the end of the house appears to be implanted into the wall of its neighbour. In the first half of this century, this roomy, double-storey terrace could have been converted into a residential, or 'reso', its verandah closed in with sheets of timber, its larger rooms partitioned, and these cramped spaces let out to people who had fallen on hard times.*

These inner-city suburbs had a reputation for toughness but, for the most part, the families who lived here did so because they were poor. Ruth Park's evocative slum classic, *The Harp in the South*, was published in 1948 and was at once enormously popular. It told a compassionate, simple story of the exuberant but disillusioned Irish-Australian Darcy family, living in their terrace house at 12½ Plymouth Street, Surry Hills, 'smelling of leaking gas, and rats, and mouldering wallpaper which had soaked up the odours of a thousand meals'. There was little sentiment for the once grandiose house, which, like its impoverished tenants, had fallen on hard times and was

> wounded with age ... The old house had perhaps been a good one in its time way back in the 'seventies. Perhaps some rich or famous person had lived there, Mama often thought, for she occasionally had the strangest feeling, as though someone delicate and fastidious and beautiful passed by her, said softly: 'This was my house. Have pity on it because it was', and vanished away again.

There was certainly no affection for the old terraces. Strident calls for their large-scale demolition

RIGHT ◆ *Dainty 'concertina' terrace houses with Juliet-sized balconies, lining a street in Sydney's Paddington.*

LEFT ✦ *'In this narrow-gutted, dirty, old house, squeezed with its elbows flat against its sides between two others, there lived seven people.'*
Ruth Park
Poor Man's Orange, *1949.*
A terrace in Redfern, Sydney, photographed during the Great Depression. Beautification and tree planting were clearly not a preoccupation, which is not at all surprising considering that times were so tough. Terraces spent much of that period unloved and uncared for, while life in a slum terrace then and later, during the housing shortage that followed World War Two, was as harsh as Ruth Park describes it in her classics of slum Sydney, The Harp in the South *and* Poor Man's Orange.

Today, almost identical houses can be found only a few suburbs away, in Little Napier Street, Paddington. Sparklingly restored and renovated, they are fashionable inner-city addresses.

came from social workers, politicians, the press, the pulpit and, with perhaps less altruistic motives, builders and developers.

To Sydney's planning authorities of the 1950s, the terrace areas were a shameful blight on the city, an embarrassing reminder of the past in a period obsessed with progress and the future. The solution for suburbs such as Paddington, Balmain, Newtown, Surry Hills and Woolloomooloo was 'demolition and replacement immediately or within 25 years'. Newspapers of the time carried photographs of architects' models of high-rise concrete flats that were to be built in The Rocks once the area had been razed.

What saved these Victorian streetscapes from the bulldozer was that priority was given to building projects creating new suburbs on semi-rural land on the cities' outskirts. Inner-city areas slipped from public attention and politicians' agendas, and remained there, out of harm's way, throughout the period of the postwar suburban sprawl. In the 1950s and early 1960s migrants from southern Europe quickly recognised terrace houses as bargain first homes in their new country. The Victorian houses were reroofed and further decay and deterioration halted. Many of the new owners had come from whitewashed villages where paint was a luxury none could afford — their houses were soon emblazoned with a riot of colour, pale blues and greens, not to mention some fearful pinks and purples.

It is not surprising that the Australian artists of this period tended to disregard the inner-city streetscapes and the rows of despised terraces. The distinctive imagery of a domestic architecture dishonoured, but still very much lived in to the point of overcrowding, was ignored until Sali Herman, a Swiss-born artist, arrived in Sydney in 1937. During the 1940s and 1950s he painted many delightful, though melancholy, canvases of the back streets of Surry Hills, Woolloomooloo and Balmain. The Director of the Art Gallery of New South Wales at the time, Will Ashton, urged him to avoid these unpopular backwaters of the

LEFT ✦ *Woolloomooloo, Sydney, c. 1870. Then as now, raised firewalls form a crisscross pattern of rooflines. Woolloomooloo was one of the slum terrace areas that Sydney's planning authorities had such big demolition plans for during the 1950s and 1960s. Fortunately, it managed to survive the vagaries of public interest and politicians' and developers' agendas. Many houses in this picture are still standing, including the row commencing at the sixth house to the right of the corner hotel, in Forbes Street, in the centre of the picture. This row of houses, with their peaky Gothic style and steep gables, is pictured on page 68.*

BELOW ✦ The French Flag, *painted by Sali Herman in 1963, has as its subject matter a group of Sydney terraces down near the wharves, probably at Woolloomooloo. Peeling paint, clothes drying on balcony clotheslines, interested watchers and the French tricolour flying the mast of an unseen ship — all create a richly textured and layered world. During the 1950s, art critics and those architects who wished to raze such areas and build a 'modern' Sydney were made uncomfortable by Herman's paintings. They were dubbed 'slumscapes'.*

city as 'such paintings would not go down well' in this country. He advised Herman to turn his eye and brush to Sydney Harbour or the bush.

Art critics and architects were also discomforted by what they described as Herman's tasteless 'slum-scapes', rows and rows of ageing houses topped by jaunty chimney pots, with curious housewives and their cats standing on the doorsteps, watching the artist at work. Terrace houses were an abomination. Politicians and architects could look the other way or dream of demolition, but Sali Herman was a realist and insisted on painting life as he saw it, not how others wished it should be. 'I had no "philosophy of slums"', he told an interviewer in 1958. 'I painted houses because houses are parts of people and people are parts of houses.' After a long and difficult road to acceptance, Sali Herman's paintings now hang in Australia's major public and State galleries.

Revivalism Revived

✦✦✦

These older suburbs were certainly colourful places and began to attract artists and actors to live in them. Paddington, with its myriad layers of peeling paint and splashes of brilliant colour, became a Sydney Montmartre, still seedy and unloved but with a bohemian, cosmopolitan atmosphere.

ABOVE ✦ *Shops were often built at the corner or end of a terrace. Allowance has been made for terraces to continue from this c. 1870 shop in Chippendale.*

In the early 1960s young couples, who had perhaps grown up in and were disillusioned with the sprawling new suburbs, began to buy terrace houses in Sydney's Paddington and Balmain and Melbourne's Parkville and Carlton. To their delight they found most of these houses, now almost a century old, to be remarkably sound in structure. Removal of the years of accumulated paint often exposed superb cedar joinery and elegant marble fireplace surrounds, which, like the houses themselves, had survived through a process of protective neglect. Most terrace houses had a small private garden, and once a new kitchen and bathroom had been installed, they proved to be very adaptable to modern, inner-city living. The sumptuousness of the nineteenth-century facades was easily exploited with paint. All in all, the effect was stunning.

The gradual move back to the terraces quickly turned into a rush. The status of these older sub-urbs underwent a startling reversal, and the process of their 'gentrification' and the subsequent spiralling in house values has been ongoing. These reborn Victorian suburbs generat-ed a new vitality. Double-fronted corner shops were converted into restaurants or galleries. The number of owner-occupied houses increased. Local shopping centres became more upmarket, the neighbour-hoods more prosperous.

As one suburb became fashionable enough to drive its house prices beyond the reach of first-home buyers, the process was repeated in neighbouring areas with large stocks of unrestored nineteenth-century houses. This pattern continues.

BELOW ❖ *Paddington's former corner grocery shops, such as this one on Windsor Street, have proved adaptable as restaurants, cafes and galleries. The dainty cantilever wrap-around balconies of the former residences above only serve to add to their charm.*

The Urban Restoration Movement

✦✦✦

The initiative for restoring Australia's Victorian heritage came from the home owners themselves. Town councils and planning authorities who, during the 1950s, wished to raze all such 'substandard housing' and build concrete blocks of flats in their place, were at first bemused by these early attempts at restoration.

It seems strange to us now that the notion of renovation instead of demolition did not even enter their thinking on the subject. However, to understand the past, we must understand the standards and values of that past. There was no nostalgia, in the 1950s, for the still very recent pre-war period of the Depression. To many, the forlorn-looking terraces held memories of hard times in squalid, over-crowded conditions, and after the added hardships of the war years, people wanted a fresh start. In housing, as in everything else, the mood was for renewal, not reversal. The past, especially the very recent past, was underrated throughout the 1950s, which may partly explain some of the mindless and brutal demolitions that did take place in this decade.

LEFT • Beautifully painted and maintained stucco and iron crown this Italianate terrace house in Kerferd Road, Albert Park, Melbourne. Note the tiny, delicate lion heads beneath the curved roof canopy. Perhaps it was this fine cast-iron pattern that first suggested the twentieth-century term, 'iron lace'.

Today, all levels of government wish to be seen as conscious and caring of the architecture of a now-vanished era, despite some of the official vandalism committed in the past.

During the 1970s and 1980s two major projects were carried out in Sydney by the Federal and State Governments to rehabilitate two virtually intact, but rapidly deteriorating, nineteenth-century urban precincts. The Federal Labor Government purchased the Glebe Estate from the Church of England for $17.5 million in 1974 . It then restored and renovated the area and its terraces to the authentic, nineteenth-century style. The New South Wales State Government's Woolloomooloo Project was a similar initiative, where the demolition orders on this historic area were reversed and its nineteenth-century character restored. In both projects sympathetic new infill terrace housing was added and long-term residents resettled in familiar locales. The professional research devoted to these projects generated a lot of new and useful information

ABOVE ✦ *A pair of post-modern terrace houses in Paddington. Blank pediments, louvred windows and lined render — minimal decoration derived from the excesses of Victorianism.*

on authentic colour schemes and other aspects of Victorian housing renewal.

However, as already mentioned, the brunt of the expense and the work involved in this spectacular Victorian urban revival that has taken place in towns and cities around Australia has been borne by terrace home owners themselves. For a person to own or to occupy a sparklingly restored terrace house indicates more than just the fulfilling of accommodation needs. It reflects a commitment to and a respect for the architectural heritage of these remaining examples of Australia's most exuberant and enduring style. Nor is this commitment confined to the individual's own home. As early as the 1960s, terrace owners had formed local associations to protect and improve the Victorian character of their streetscapes as a whole.

Today, there are numerous books available on all aspects of domestic heritage conservation, and each

ABOVE ✦ *'As nature is beautiful, ornamental details derived immediately from beautiful natural objects must ensure a beautiful design.'* Ralph N. Wornum Analysis of Ornament, 1856. *Ornamental designs that incorporated birds and flowers pervaded Victorian fashion and the decorative arts. Ladies wore aviaries of feathers on their hats, and floral designs were popular in domestic decoration, both internal and external. Arum lilies are rendered in cast iron on this rare baluster panel in Short Street, Bendigo.*

capital city has specialist shops and services offering reproduction or recycled cast ironwork, brassware, tiles, joinery, and plaster and cement casts.

There are some important concepts to consider before beginning to restore a terrace house. One is that the owners of the houses in a terrace row should try to reach a consensus on a uniform and traditional colour scheme. This is never easy, as not everyone will have the same ideas and financial resources. But, if the goodwill is present, it can be regarded as a long-term project; one that will ultimately increase the appeal, and the resale value, of all the houses in the row.

Unsympathetic 'renovations', such as installing sliding aluminium windows, enclosing balconies, overpainting feature brickwork, or using pseudo-antique aluminium iron lace panels, should be avoided. By spending a little more — for example, on aluminium panels that are accurate reproductions and, when painted, are indistinguishable from the originals — the visual impact will be improved out of all proportion to the extra cost. It is also likely to increase the property's value. The trend is towards authentic restoration, and a discriminating house buyer will realise that reversing unsympathetic 'improvements' is more expensive than restoring a house whose character remains essentially intact.

BELOW ✦ *Ellimatta is a symmetrical terrace-style house in Drummond Street, Carlton. Its deep arching brackets, so characteristic of the Melbourne style of terrace, have been lovingly restored. The ironwork has a matching motif that flows from the brackets to the balcony panels.*

The Golden Light
of Nostalgia

◆◆◆

Age, nostalgia and exalted real estate values have thrown a golden light over many of the terrace areas in Australian cities, especially Sydney and Melbourne. However, gentrification has not reached all the streets of the inner city. Some are shabby and their terraces more than a little rundown, but the rents are cheap and it's close to the city.

Other suburbs, such as Paddington, Balmain and Carlton, have undergone several waves of renovation over the past five decades, each one leaving its high-tide mark on the facades or the interiors of the terraces — the Mediterranean-influenced 1950s, the raffish, bohemian 1960s and 1970s, the prim, restoration-conscious 1980s, and the lifestyle-driven 1990s. During the 1960s and 1970s many terraces had their exterior skin of stucco removed to reveal the rich

RIGHT ◆ *Trousers on sale for 4 shillings, 9 pence and shirts for 1 shilling, 3 pence in the window of J. S. Law's drapery shop in Balmain, c. 1890. Though built of brick, it has render on the balcony, lined to resemble stone. This building was erected free-standing but with a possible view to having a terrace of houses or shops built to its right on the same alignment.*

90

RIGHT ✦ *This terrace at 74 Park Street, South Yarra, has a strikingly original 'opera box' design. This would have been custom-made by the foundry that supplied the cast iron. Custom-designed ironwork is rare. Victorians generally preferred novelty to individuality in domestic ornament.*

colours and textures of the porous sandstock bricks behind. Inside, incongruous arches of recycled sand-stocks were built across the shag-pile carpeted floors of former Victorian parlours. Some prime terraces have been renovated up to three times by now, some culminating in the interior being completely gutted for a nineties-style post-modern reconstruction in glass and steel, with a dazzling atrium.

Terrace house living is quintessential inner city living — compact and close, against the backdrop of its own architectural charm and ornamented display. It is a long way from the more suburban Australian dream of a home on a quarter-acre block. And it is very fashionable.

Cliff Hardy, the protagonist in Peter Corris's crime novels, lives in a rundown Glebe terrace, strug-gling to pay off his mortgage on lean pickings as a Sydney private detective. In *White Meat*, Hardy gives his cynically envious, through-the-car-windscreen musings on the terrace house as he cruises the streets of Paddington:

> Almost every house in the street had been restored to its former glory with glistening black iron lace standing out against the virgin white paint jobs. The gardens were deep for terraces and there was enough bamboo in them to build a *kampong*.

Today's resplendent terraces feature in television dramas, commercials and films, unmistakably identi-fying the city and declaring the social status of its occupants. They are also frequently the subject of arti-cles in lifestyle and interior decorating magazines, which, more than anything else, continue the trend of their ongoing fashionableness.

A century has passed since the apogee of Victorianism, when the cycle of the terrace's decline and renewal commenced. We have now come full cir-cle. Terrace houses are amongst the most sought-after, prestigious homes in Australian cities. They provide

RIGHT ◆ *'Woolloomooloo' in the local Aboriginal language is said to mean 'Where are you going?' Until the 1970s the 'Loo and its nineteenth-century streetscapes seemed destined for decrepitude and the developer's bulldozer. The New South Wales Government's Woolloomooloo Project happily reversed that direction. Houses such as these terraces in Forbes Street were refurbished and the facades restored to their original colours. Then the residents were resettled in the area. And like the Victorian taste in ornament, the names of the colours of the Victorian palette were exotic, Eau-de-Nil and Venetian Red being but two examples.*

a much-needed form of urban consolidation, giving a balance between the two extremes of the 'sacred' quarter-acre block and the sprawling, unserviceable metropolis it creates, and the land-economic but very dehumanising high-rise. In a skyline increasingly under siege from monoliths, the charm and exuberance of our cities' terrace houses are irresistible, forming a reassuring and enduring link with the past.

BIBLIOGRAPHY

The following titles were consulted in the preparation of this book and can be recommended as further reading on various aspects of the history and development of Australian terraces.

Apperly, Richard et al. *A Pictorial Guide to Identifying Australian Architecture*. Sydney: Angus & Robertson, 1989.

Boyd, Robin. *Australia's Home: Why Australians Built the Way They Did*, 2nd edn. Melbourne: Melbourne University Press, 1987.

Cannon, Michael. *The Land Boomers*. Melbourne: Melbourne University Press, 1978.

——*Life in the Cities* (Australia in the Victorian Age, vol. 3). Melbourne: Thomas Nelson, 1978.

Casey, M. *Early Melbourne Architecture*, 3rd edn. Melbourne: Oxford University Press, 1975.

Crook, J. Mordaunt. *The Dilemma of Style*, 2nd edn. London: John Murray, 1989.

Dixon, Roger and Muthesius, Stefan. *Victorian Architecture*, 2nd edn. London: Thames and Hudson, 1978.

Evans, Ian. *The Australian Home*. Sydney: Flannel Flower Press, 1983.

——*Restoring Old Houses: A Guide to Authentic Restoration*, 3rd edn. Melbourne: Sun Books, 1989.

Evans, Ian et al. *Colour Schemes for Old Australian Houses*. Sydney: Flannel Flower Press, 1984.

Fitzgerald, Shirley. *Rising Damp: Sydney 1870–1890*. Melbourne: Oxford University Press, 1987.

Fowles, Joseph. *Sydney in 1848*. Annotated facsimile edn. Sydney: Ure Smith, 1962.

Fraser, Hugh and Joyce, Ray. *The Federation House: Australia's Own Style*. Sydney: Lansdowne Press, 1986.

Freeland, J. M. *Architecture in Australia: A History*. Melbourne: Penguin, 1972.

Gloag, John. *Victorian Taste*, 2nd edn. Newton Abbot: David & Charles, 1979.

Irving, Robert (ed.). *The History and Design of the Australian House*. Melbourne: Oxford University Press, 1985.

Kelly, Max. *Paddock Full of Houses: Paddington 1840–1890*. Paddington: Doak Press, 1978.

——*Faces of the Street: William Street Sydney 1916*. Paddington: Doak Press, 1982.

Lambert, Susan (ed.). *Pattern and Design*. Exhibition catalogue. London: Victoria and Albert Museum, 1983.

Molyneux, Ian. *Looking Around Perth: A Guide to the Architecture of Perth and Surrounding Towns*. East Fremantle: Westcolour Press, 1981.

Muthesius, Stefan. *The English Terraced House*. New Haven: Yale University Press, 1982.

Park, Ruth. *Poor Man's Orange*. Melbourne: Penguin Books, 1980.

——*The Harp in the South*. Melbourne: Penguin Books, 1982.

Pearce, Barry. *Sali Herman: Retrospective 1981*. Catalogue. Sydney: Art Gallery of New South Wales, 1981.

Pikusa, Stefan. *The Adelaide House, 1836–1901*. Adelaide: Wakefield Press, 1986.

Robertson, E. G. *Victorian Heritage: Ornamental Cast Iron in Architecture*. Melbourne: Georgian House, 1960.

Robertson, E. G. and Robertson, J. *Parkville*. Melbourne: Georgian House, 1975.

Smith, Bernard and Smith, Kate. *The Architectural Character of Glebe*, 2nd edn. Sydney: Sydney University Press, 1989.

Summerson, John. *Georgian London*. London: Pleiades Books, 1945.

Turner, Brian. *Australia's Iron Lace*. Sydney: Allen and Unwin, 1985.

Woolcock, Steve and Fisher, Rod. *Petrie-Terrace: Brisbane 1858–1988*. Brisbane: Boolarong Publications, 1988.

PERMISSIONS

The publisher would like to thank the following people or organisations for permission to reproduce material:

Melbourne University Press, for the quotes on pages 9 and 12, from Robin Boyd, *Australia's Home*, MUP, 1952; the estate of Patrick White, for the quote on page 15, from Patrick White, *Voss*, 1957; Kemalde Pty Ltd, C/- Curtis Brown (Aust) Pty Ltd Sydney, for the quotes on page 80, from Ruth Park, *The Harp in the South*, Penguin Books, 1982, and page 81, from Ruth Park, *Poor Man's Orange*, Penguin Books, 1980; Peter Corris, for the quote on page 92, from Peter Corris, *White Meat*, Pan, 1981.

PICTURE CREDITS

All photographs are by Brian Turner (© Brian Turner), except those listed below, which were supplied and reproduced with the permission of the following people or organisations:

p. 3, Council of the City of Sydney; p. 10, Museum of Victoria Photographic Archive Project; p. 14, Ray Jarrett; p. 16, S. Muthesius, University of East Anglia, Norwich, Great Britain; p. 18, Royal Commission on the Historical Monuments of England; p. 20, Historic Photograph Resource Centre; p. 22 (top), Mitchell Library; p. 22 (bottom), Mitchell Library; p. 23, New South Wales Government Printer; pp. 28–29, New South Wales Government Printer; p. 43, Council of the City of Sydney; p. 46, Council of the City of Sydney; p. 47, Council of the City of Sydney; p. 50, Council of the City of Sydney; p. 51, New South Wales Government Printer; p. 57, Council of the City of Sydney; p. 58 (bottom), John Oxley Library, Brisbane; p. 61, Council of the City of Sydney; p. 67 (bottom), J. Mordaunt Crook; p. 76, Waverley Council; p. 78, Council of the City of Sydney; p. 81, Council of the City of Sydney; p. 82, Council of the City of Sydney; p. 83, Barry Pearce, The Sali Herman Estate; p. 84, Council of the City of Sydney; p. 86, Ray Jarrett; p. 89, Ray Jarrett; p. 90, Mitchell Library.

PHOTO CAPTIONS
Front cover: 1870s terrace, St Vincent Place, Albert Park, Melbourne
Page 1: End terrace, Chapman Street, North Melbourne
Page 2: Ellen's Terrace, Carlton, Melbourne
Page 3: Foveaux Street, Surry Hills, Sydney, 1909
Page 5: Former corner shop, Shadforth Street, Paddington, Sydney
Pages 6–7: Alpha Terrace, Launceston, Tasmania

INDEX